MAN SPRES SIONS

MANSPRESSIONS: DECODING MEN'S BEHAVIOR

First Printing, July 14, 2015

All text is © Joe Biel and Elly Blue

This edition is © Microcosm Publishing, 2015

Layout, design, and illustrations by Meggyn Pomerleau

Body text is set in Baskerville

Microcosm Publishing

2752 N. Williams Ave

Portland, OR 97227

For a catalog, write or visit

MicrocosmPublishing.com

ISBN 978-1-62106-898-3

This is Microcosm #195

Distributed worldwide by Legato / Perseus and Turnaround in the UK.

This book was printed on post-consumer paper in the U. S.

MANSPRESSIONS
DECODING MEN'S BEHAVIOR

JOE BIEL & ELLY BLUE

DANGER KEY:

Variations of mustaches are located at the bottom of each page.
Their significance can be found within this key.

Clueless & Annoying

Entitled & Demanding

Ready to Wreak Serious Havoc

Plotting Against You

Has Already Burned Your Village

MANTRODUCTION

I t has been a hallmark of the annals of performativity theory in the past 45 years that gender performance at the feminine end of the spectrum has received tremendous attention, aiming to make up for many decades prior of scholarly misconstrual and dismissiveness. Femininity continues to be explored in-depth, observed, recorded, dissected, critiqued, reproduced, celebrated, mocked, defended, defined, and contested. It seems that the project of figuring women out is a fascinating one among our fellow researchers.

And no wonder! We, your humble authors, spend as much time as anyone wondering what the hell makes women tick. Truly it is one of the world's great mysteries.

Predictably though, when we combed through the *British Journal of Masculinity Studies*[1] or even dug through the course catalog for Cornell University, where the nation's first women's studies program was introduced in 1969, there was barely any mention, let alone analysis of men's masked social expressionism or examination of the non-verbal expressions that men use to express their lack of confidence while babbling on about every subject under the sun.

Discovery of this glaring omission has fixed a question firmly into the forefront of our minds ever since:

What about the men?

We set about answering this question, indeed righting this wrong, with diligence and attention.

---

1. B.J. Masc. Stud. 1877-1988

All of the examples in this volume have been gathered in the field, in real situations involving real people deploying manspressions.

Some instances were quite easy to collect: A **manologue** provides ample leisure time during which detailed observations may be recorded. But other research environments, such as events where large quantities of men were in a concentrated space and time was limited, had us struggling to keep up as fleeting moments of manspression poured in faster than we could observe, giggle about, and write them down.

Because of the nature of manspressions, which tend to be interpreted by performers and observers alike as natural and normal, at times we were only able to identify and define terms in later discourse and research. "What's the manspression for that?" we would ask each other after it came to us that a certain encounter had been of this typology.

Many hours were spent analyzing word origins, definitions, male behavior patterns, gaps in existing language, explained phenomena, and of course, claims about the *oppression of men.*

It is worth noting that manspression is limited neither to the biologically male nor to those with an outwardly male gender expression. Like any cultural formation, this one can be picked up, with greater or lesser success, by any person. In fact, we have noted that it is quite common to find non-men engaging in manspression in one form or another. This is unsurprising upon reflection, as considerable personal and societal power is maintained and transmitted by such behaviors. If you don't spend too much time thinking about it, male behaviors can seem pretty cool, though the price to be paid for indulging in them is often steep.

In all cases we have done our best to represent these cultural structures and behaviors as accurately as possible, but our experience is limited and our geographic reach does not extend beyond certain areas of the U.S.

In short: More research is needed, more depth can surely be achieved. We hope you agree that we have built a solid foundation in an important yet neglected field of study, and we encourage you to build on it. We confess that our research has an activist aim as well—that the men of the world may now enjoy the scrutiny that their female counterparts have been neigh well monopolizing for many a decade.

We look forward to hearing about your follow-up research, works, and conclusion. Please contact us and direct your MAN FAIL (that is our own abbreviation for the awkward technical term "manspressions: feedback about idiomatic language") to our address in the back of this book.

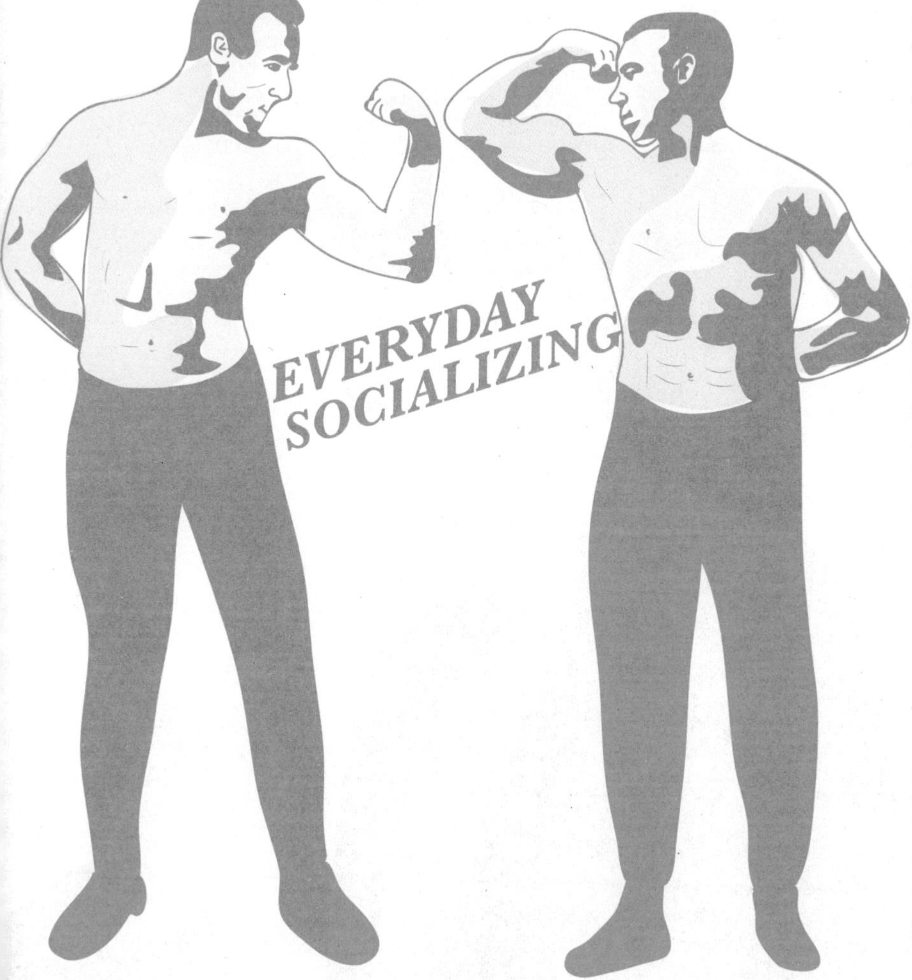

EVERYDAY SOCIALIZING

MANSPLAIN

To lecture someone on a topic that they know quite a lot about, as though they in fact know nothing.

Pro tip:
Ask lots of questions. Enjoy the show.

MANSPLANATION

A basic outline of your own area of expertise,
delivered to you in a lecturing tone.

MANOLOGUE
A man is talking. Resistance is futile.

Pro tip:
Always carry a book for boredom…or
when you need a blunt object.

MANVERSATION
Two men are talking, nobody is listening.

MANSTACHE

Identifies, protects, and defends his masculinity.

MANSWERS

Mansplanations with a brief, off-hand delivery.

see page 11

MANSGRESSIONS
Crimes against masculinity

MANCOURAGEMENT

Men leading other men to misbehave

MANBASSADOR

A man who takes it upon himself to be your guide.

MANSERTATION

A depthy treatise on a topic which cannot be too small. Typically delivered on a date, at a bus stop, or in other situations where the audience is captive.

MANPIRE

He consistently sucks all life from the room and, quite possibly, from your life.

Pro tip:
Leave this one to the professionals.

MANTISTE

An artist with a vision—at least, he won't stop talking about how he has one.

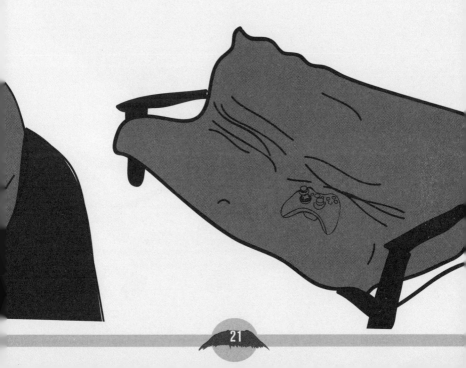

ARGUMANT

Citing the opinions of "most people" to create a sense of authority on a topic without the assistance of evidence or data.

Pro tip: Do not, we repeat, do not engage or escalate. Walk away.

YAAAAAAA

DUUUUUDE

MANBREVIATION

A series of grunts, looks, and gestures that convey manspression without risking the responsibility of words.

23

MANQUIPMENT

The essentials for a camping trip—assuming, of course, that someone else is bringing the toilet paper, bedding, and food.

MANSION

He describes it as his castle, but it looks more like a mancave to you.

MANIFICENCE
From his throne, he surveys his kingdom.

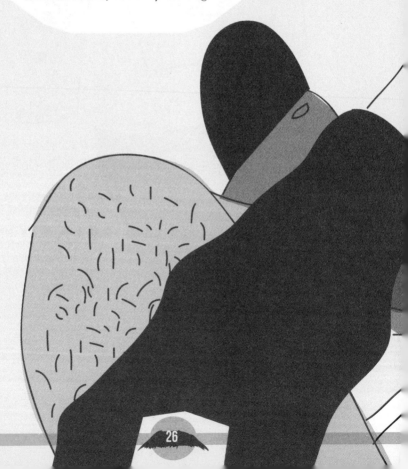

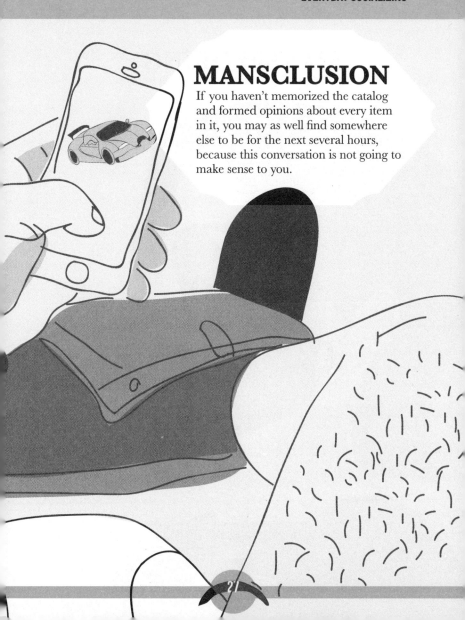

MANSCLUSION

If you haven't memorized the catalog and formed opinions about every item in it, you may as well find somewhere else to be for the next several hours, because this conversation is not going to make sense to you.

MANSPLORING

No maps. Off-road. Just don't mention that he's lost.

Pro tip: Bring some snacks.

MANSPORTATION

It's not designed to carry kids or groceries, and
no, he's too busy to take you to the airport.

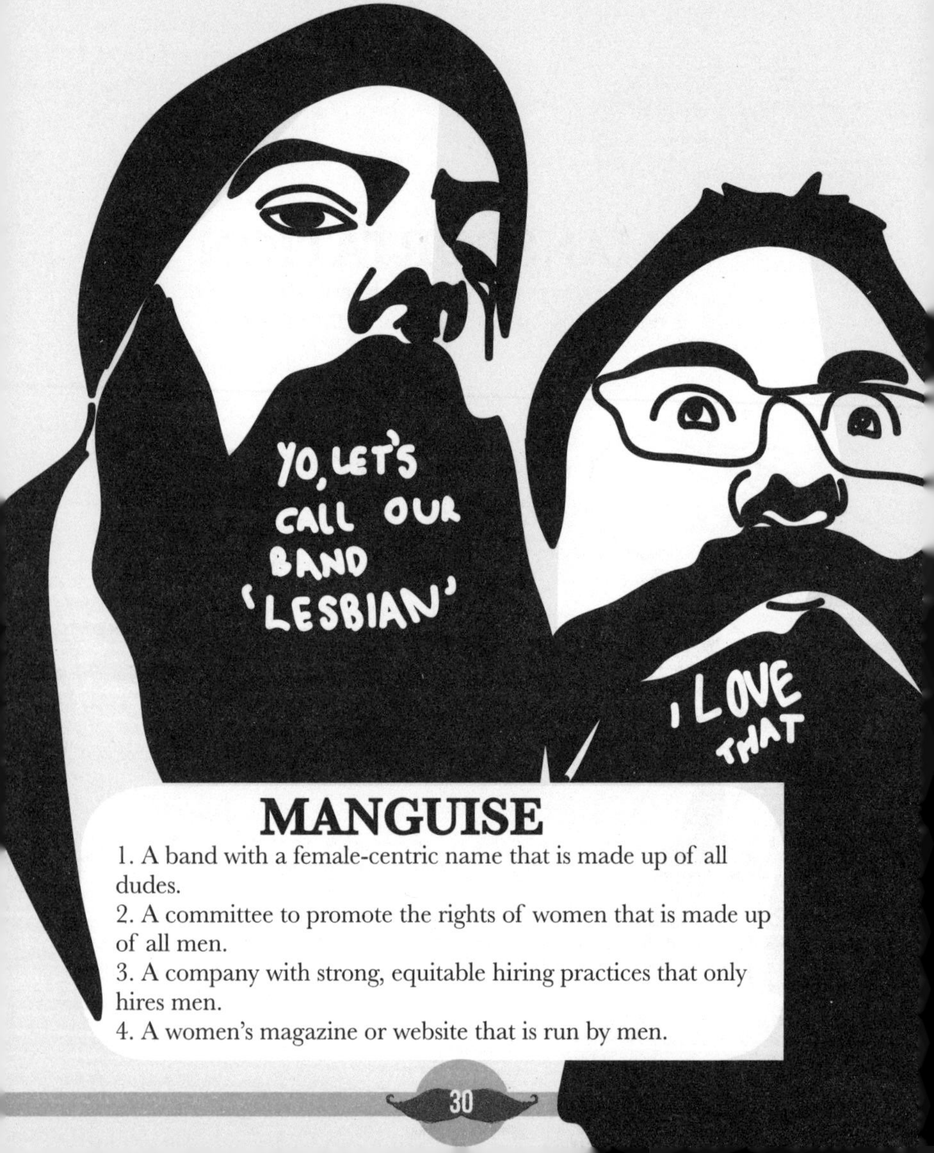
YO, LET'S CALL OUR BAND 'LESBIAN'
I LOVE THAT

MANGUISE

1. A band with a female-centric name that is made up of all dudes.
2. A committee to promote the rights of women that is made up of all men.
3. A company with strong, equitable hiring practices that only hires men.
4. A women's magazine or website that is run by men.

MANCABULARY

1. Words of excessive length that could easily be replaced by simpler ones.
2. A gross misuse of words.
3. Words that have no meaning.

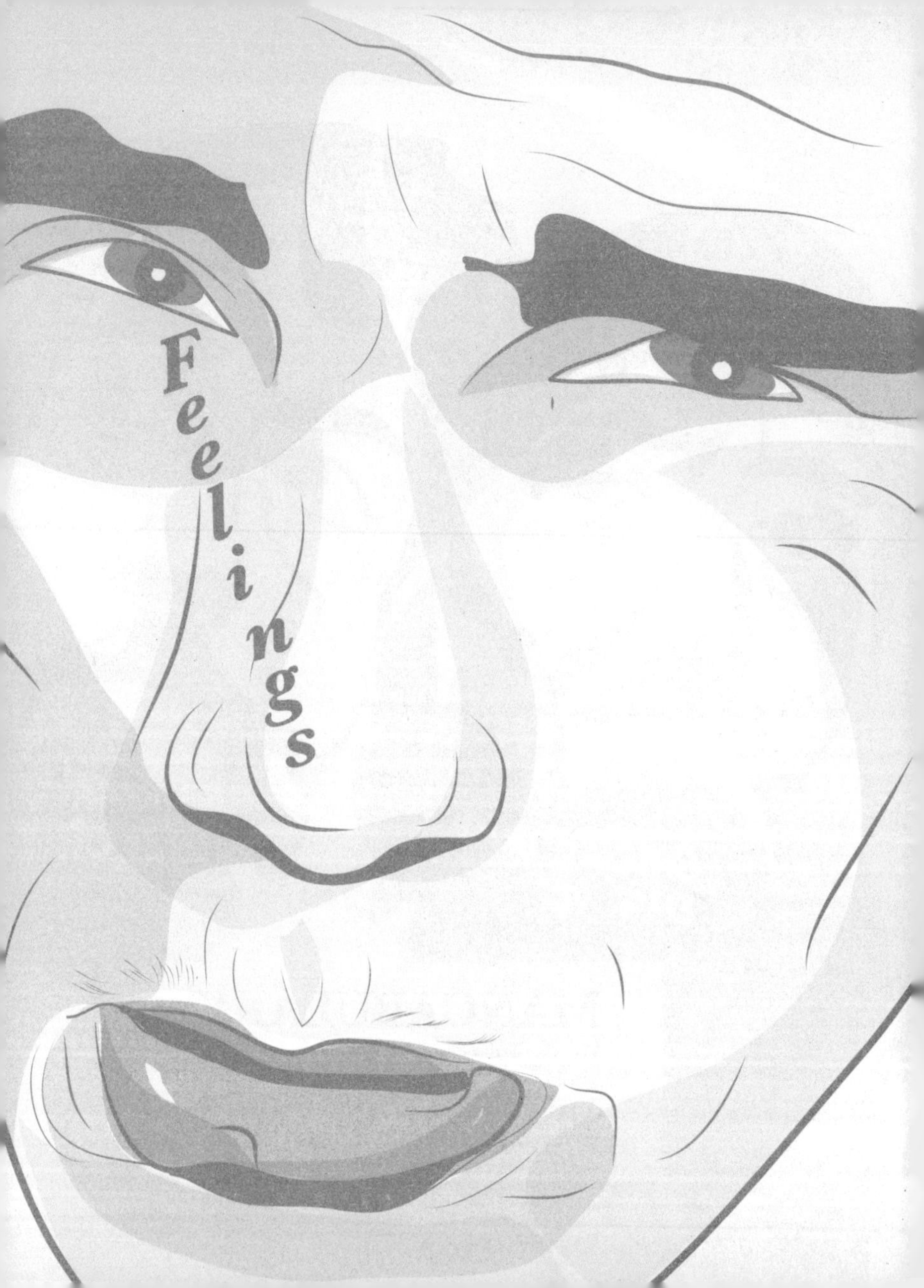
Feelings

MANSECURITY

He feels judged by your choices in life and will go to any length to defend himself. Jobs, family, dating, where you live, how you get around—he can't help but feel it's all a reflection on him. His mission is to keep you from doing it, or at least from enjoying it.

Pro tip: Remember that your choices are about you, not about him.

MANDESCENDING

1. He reduces your self-esteem to match his own with statements like "we are both getting so out of shape."
2. He is willing to join you at the level he perceives you at...that's about a third grade level, right?

MANSQUERADE

He's *such* a sensitive guy.
In fact he'll tell you all about it.

I'D OFFER YOU A BITE, BUT YOU'RE WATCHING YOUR WEIGHT... RIGHT? I KNOW HOW HEALTHY WOMEN TRY TO BE.

Pro tip: FLEE!

MANSPLOSION

He can't talk about his feelings, which makes them ten times as destructive when he does let them out. Just try to get out of the room in time.

MANTOXIFICATION

A contagious disease transmitted when a man
suddenly dumps his feelings onto you.

Pro tip:
Never come back.

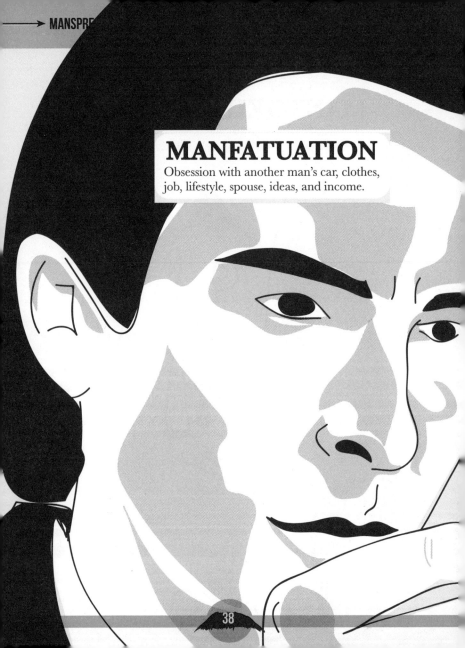

MANFATUATION

Obsession with another man's car, clothes, job, lifestyle, spouse, ideas, and income.

Pro tip:
Initialize stare of death.

MANTERCEPTION

When women are discussing sexist
experiences and a man jumps in
to dominate the conversation to
explain that *he* isn't like that.

#notallmen

MANDATE

The ends justify the means. Bold attempts must be made and no price is too high, so long as he isn't the one paying it.

(see also: manifest destiny)

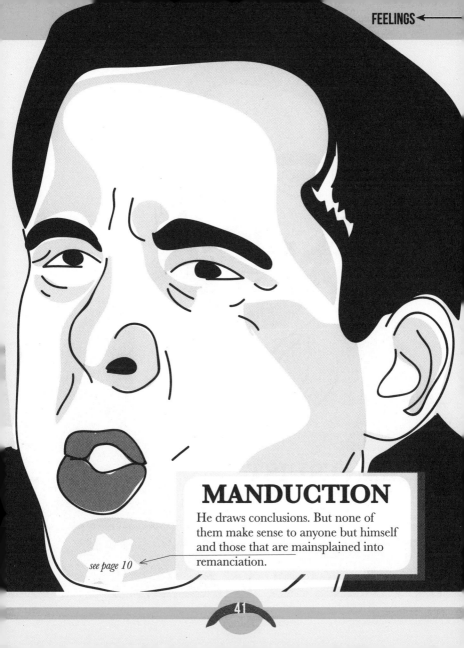

MANDUCTION

He draws conclusions. But none of them make sense to anyone but himself and those that are mainsplained into remanciation.

see page 10 ←

MANTRUIST

Better not criticize this guy. You don't want to discourage him from all the good works he does for the world.

MANQUEST

It sounds like he is asking for permission, but he is in fact informing you of what is about to happen.

MANVERSION

He has seen the light!
Are you ready to hear all about it?

MAN SEQUITUR

What were we talking about again?
Oh yeah, me!

MANEUVERING

That bewildering chain of events when you explain to a man how he has upset you and five minutes later you find yourself comforting his wounded feelings.

MANDIGNATION

When society's persecution of men requires someone to speak up!

DISMANBIGUATION

Your argument, while distressingly accurate in the big picture, may omit one or two tangential details which, fortunately, he is happy to clear up for you in depth.

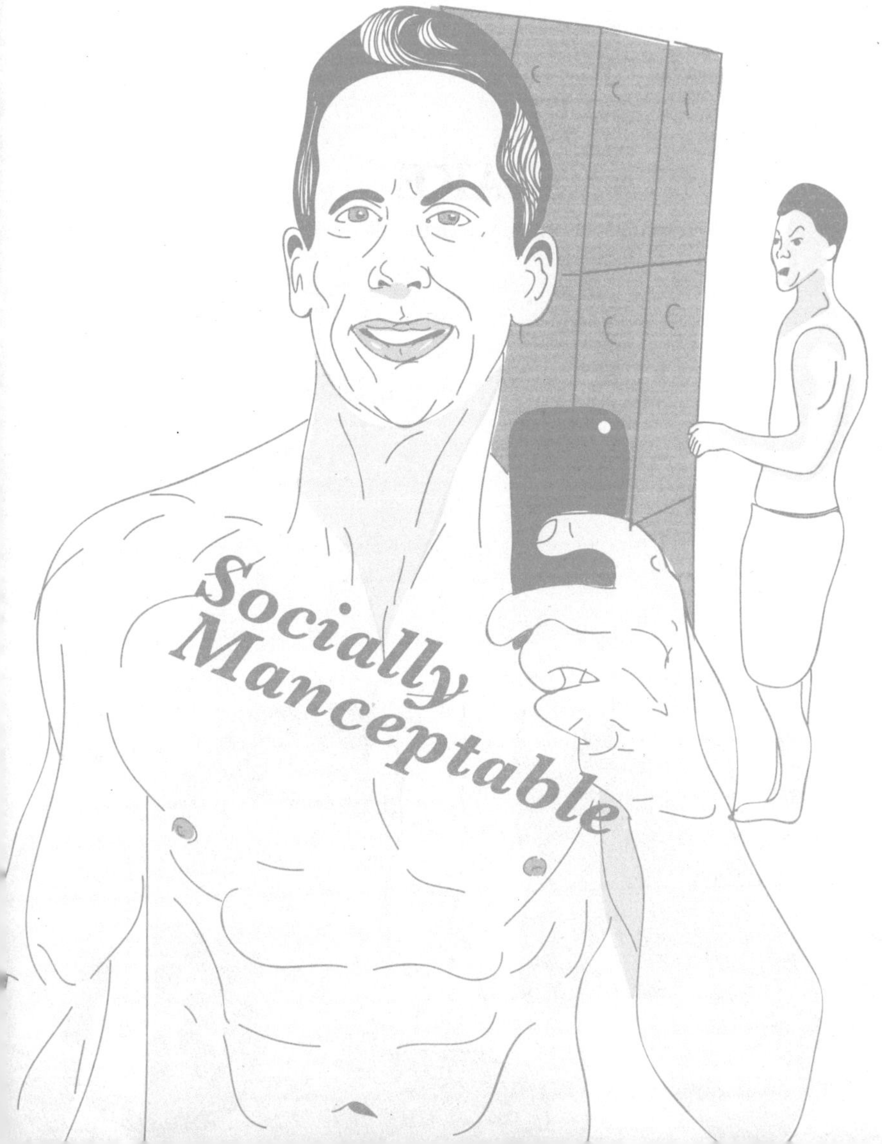
Socially
Manceptable

MANSTAKE

There is no such thing as a manstake.

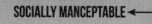

Pro tip:
Flee! You don't owe him anything.

MANSUASION

What do you mean you don't want to?
Of course you want to.

MANGNORANCE
Everyone has blind spots, though some
are more unbelievable than others.

MANTHROPOLOGY

1. Back in prehistoric times, men went out and hunted alone while women stayed home and worked together to cook food and raise the children. "It's only natural, baby."

2. Detailed observations on almost any subject, delivered in paragraph form.

MANTHENTICITY

He's happy to whip up dinner on the grill, but he sure as hell won't clean up afterwards.

MANSTALGIA

"Those were the good old days, when men were men and women were women."

MANFLUENCED

Only accepting men's input and
opinions as valid or credible

MANSTINCT

Everyone knows you can't trust facts. That's why he follows his gut, which is far more reliable than any kind of empirical evidence.

MANSTREAM

The standard for what is considered normal, often passed down by manstitutions, mannentators, and manthropologists.

see pages 92, 69, and 53

MANTIFICATION

"Not that I actually believe this, but someone has to be the Devil's Advocate."

MANTRARIAN

He loves to contradict everything that you say, even in contradiction to his prior statements.

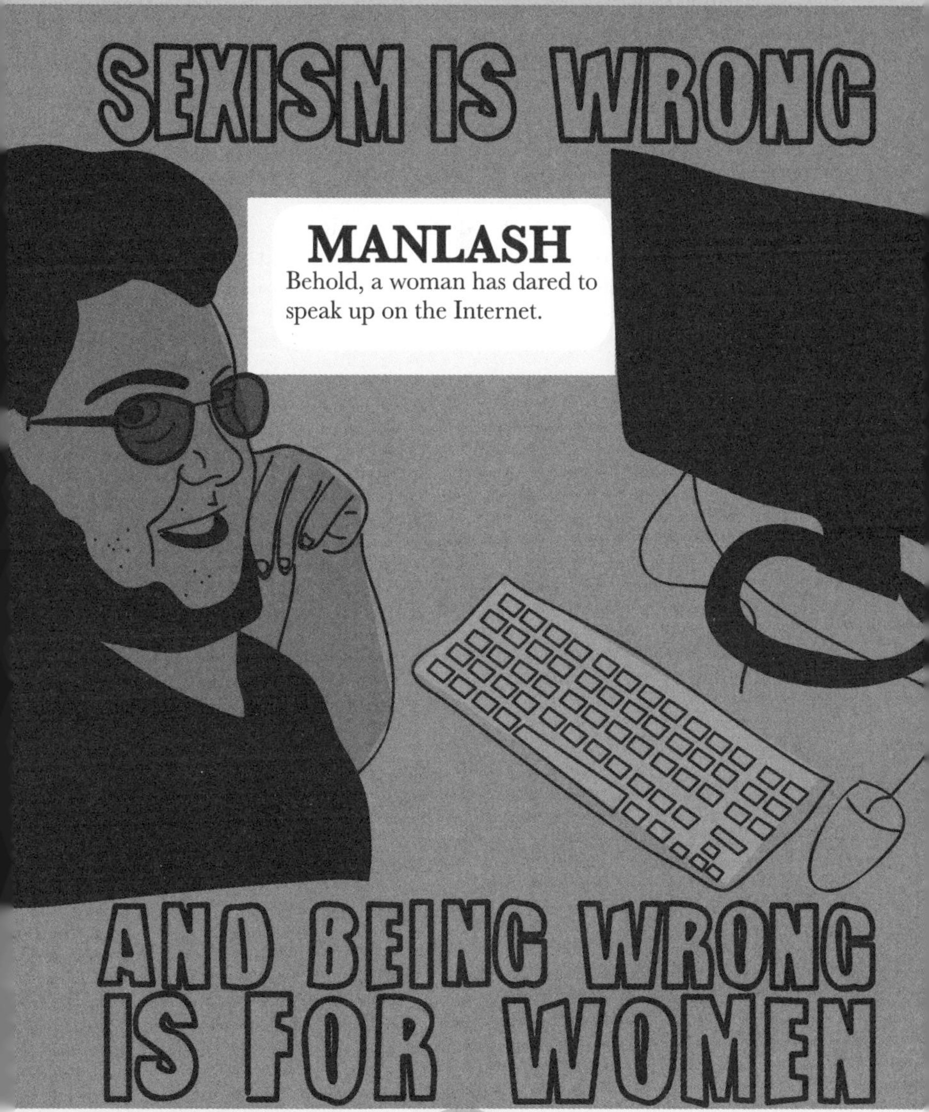
SEXISM IS WRONG
MANLASH
Behold, a woman has dared to speak up on the Internet.
AND BEING WRONG IS FOR WOMEN

MANTOLERANCE

He is totally okay with things that don't affect him or are outside of his locus of control. From "It's great that you won." To "I totally don't mind that the President is a woman."

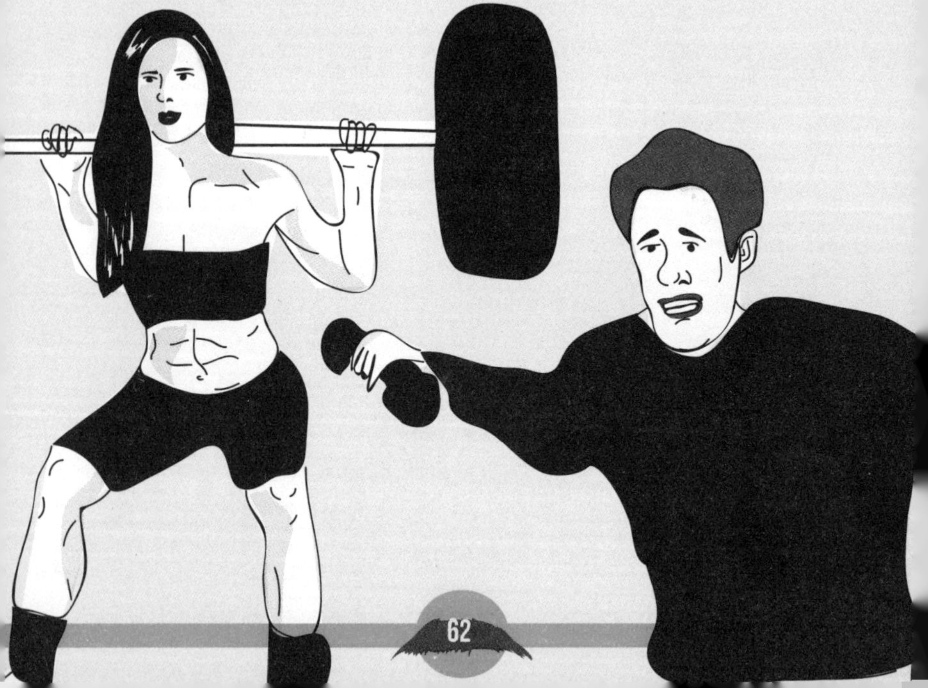

MANLUSION

The widespread belief in the benevolence and morality of the rule of men.

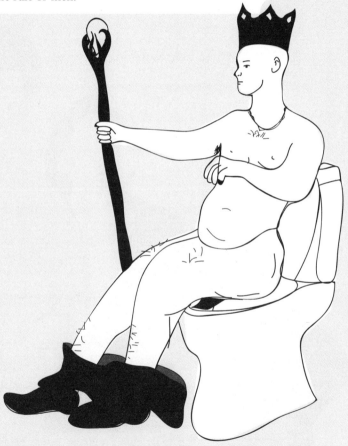

MANEO "I saw that this was an all-women event, so I thought I'd drop by and show my support."

Pro tip: Just show him the door.

MANTELLIGENT

So much more intelligent than you.

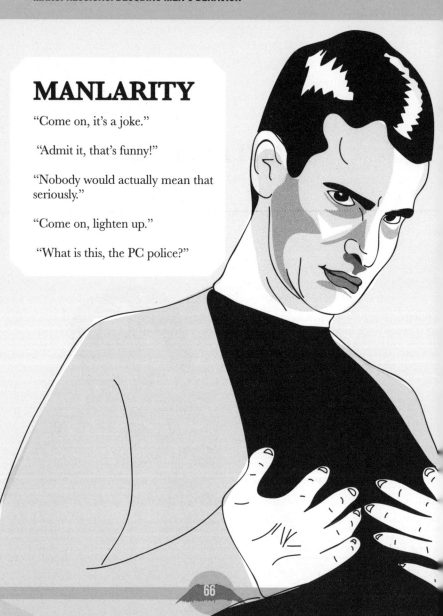

MANLARITY

"Come on, it's a joke."

"Admit it, that's funny!"

"Nobody would actually mean that seriously."

"Come on, lighten up."

"What is this, the PC police?"

MANTRUM
He can dish it out, but he can't take it.

Pro tip:
Earplugs are advisable.

MANSUMPTION

A common mistake that anyone could make.
Like thinking that the doctor is a man, or that a random woman on the street will appreciate hearing about how beautiful she looks today.

I THOUGHT MY PRIMARY CARE DOC ONLY RECOMMENDED MALE DOCTORS!

MANNENTATOR

He may appear to be a troll, but he's actually just very passionate about this topic. Known to demonstrate the mantrum.

see page 67

MANTASY

"I was raised by women, I've spent my career helping women. I'm not just a feminist; I'm an expert. So can we agree that it's pretty silly of you to question my behavior?"

MANGRY

Beware his wrath.
Seriously, be very far away.

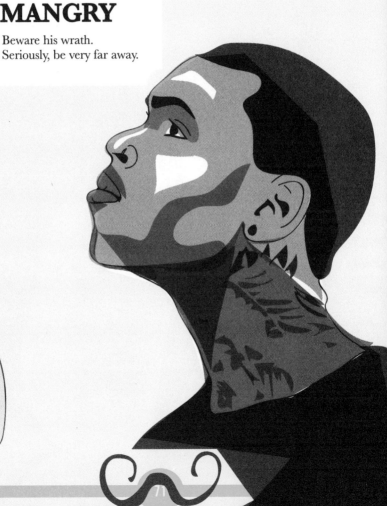

Dating

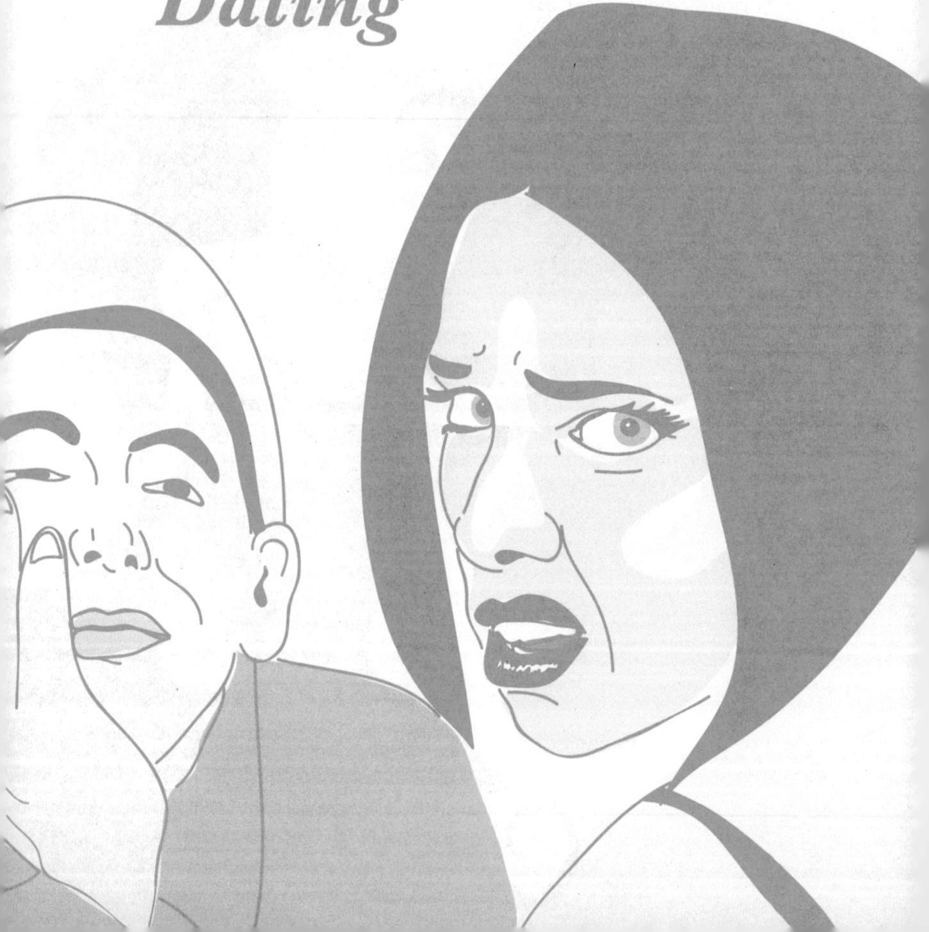

ROMANCE

Selfishly pursuing without
reciprocation or reason

**Pro tip: Oddly enough, responding
with cartoonish levels of
enthusiasm normally intimidates
him and scares him off.**

MANUAL

A collection of useless and boring trivia brought out at every party or gathering, packaged to appear interesting.

MANPORTUNITY

You didn't ask but he informs you that yes,
his big feet mean that other things are big too.

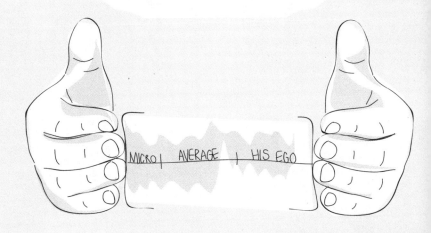

MICRO | AVERAGE | HIS EGO

Pro tip:
Always carry a magnifying glass.

MANVITATION

After being thoroughly annoying, a man invites himself to your phone number.

MANTITLEMENT

He did everything by the book, so please explain why you won't sleep with him?

EMALE

Sending unsolicited
naked photos, usually
to your work account.

Pro tip:
Forward them to his mom.

MANDSOME

"No really, don't you think I'm good looking?"

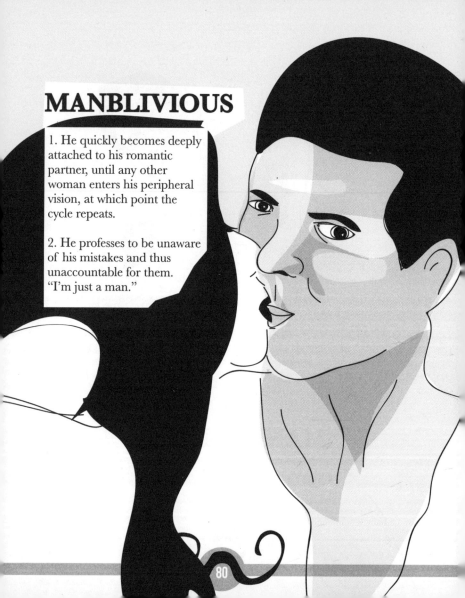

MANBLIVIOUS

1. He quickly becomes deeply attached to his romantic partner, until any other woman enters his peripheral vision, at which point the cycle repeats.

2. He professes to be unaware of his mistakes and thus unaccountable for them. "I'm just a man."

MANOPOLIZE
To understand and discuss an issue only as it relates to him.

MANTERRUPTION

He keeps talking over you but somehow his preciously rehearsed speech isn't getting the results that it did in the mirror.

MANTIC

Hijinks intended to impress you.

MENANIGANS

Mantics as a way of life, performed as a group.

→ *see page 83*

MANSPARENCY

Sometimes he makes the mistake of
telling you what he's really thinking.

MANTACIZE

"If I weren't such a nice guy, all the hot chicks would want me."

Pro tip:
Be well versed in the tactics of the Pick Up Artists and be prepared to evade them.

MANGICIAN

Days have passed since he cast his spell, and then decades, and you are still wondering how he tricked you into doing his bidding.

Pro tip:
A counter-spell can break the curse.

MANDEPENDENCE

The inherent right of a man to make choices unimpeded by any external factors.

MANFLUENCE

A condition that results from too much exposure to manspression. Symptoms include a cloudy head, extreme self-doubt, and the habit of turning statements into questions. Typically clears up in a few hours to a few months after withdrawing from exposure.

Pro tip: Take a deep breath and count to...a really high number.

Management

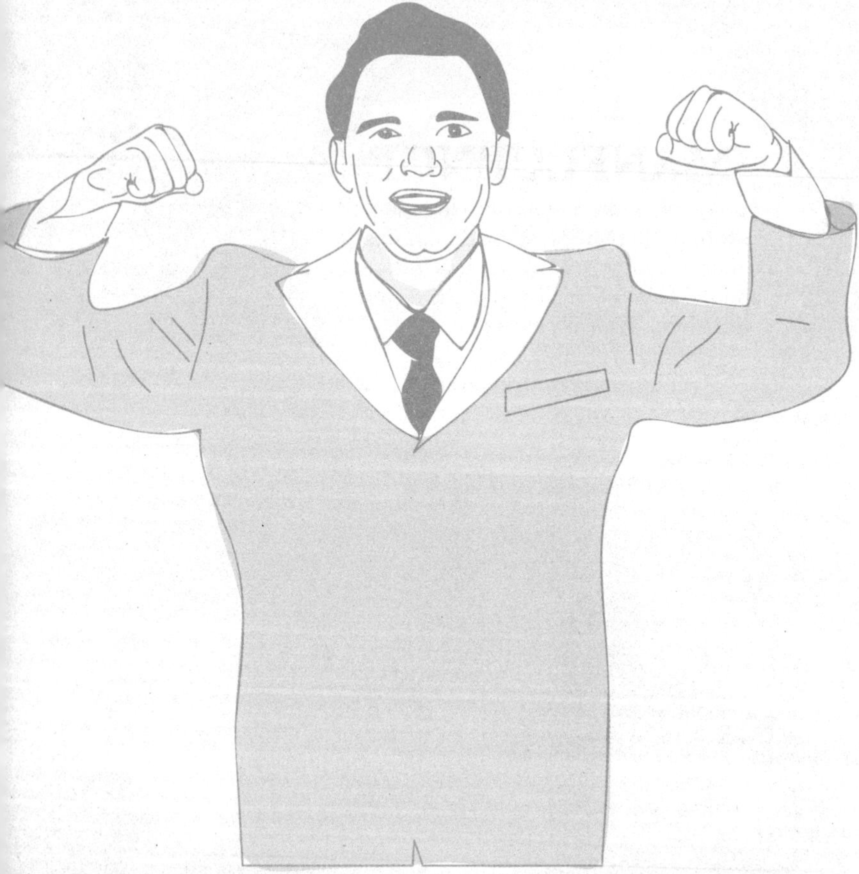

MANPROPRIATION

Your idea is so brilliant that he is getting a raise for it.

Pro tip:
Document everything.

MANSTITUTION

They run the world.

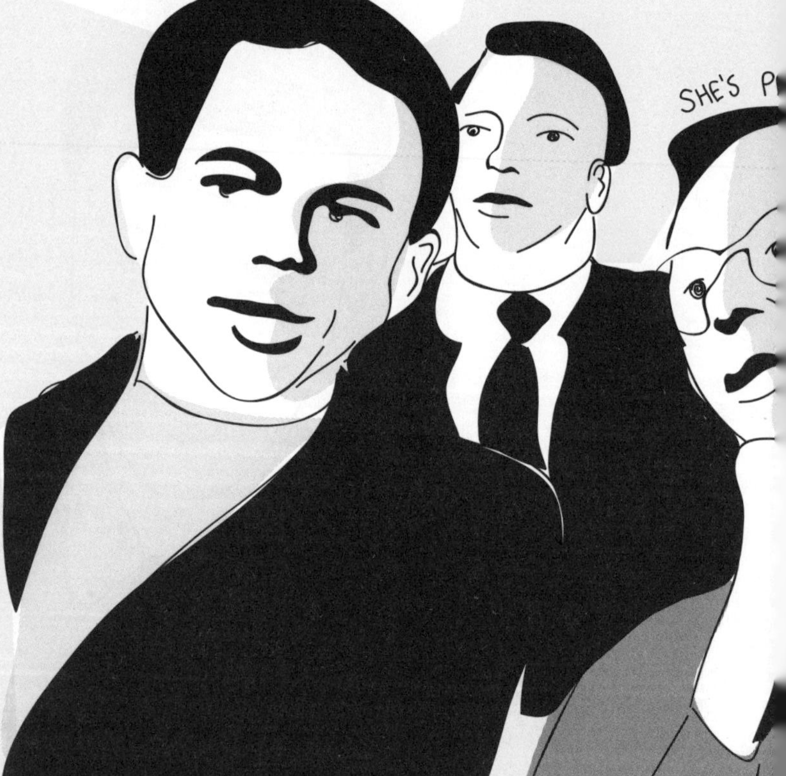
SHE'S P

MANSTABLISHMENT

Looking to advance your career?
Sorry, sister, you chose the wrong field.

MANNOYING

Were you saying something?
Because he probably didn't hear it.

MANTERVIEW

It is necessary to hire people who are not only qualified for the job but who will be a good cultural fit for the company and the team. Therefore, you will be evaluated based on a combination of your skills, your attire, your laid-back demeanor, your willingness to work nights and weekends, and your ability to take a joke.

MANFUSION

1. Your idea has suddenly been absorbed into his idea, creating a complex and not entirely successful mixture of flavors

2. You used to understand this issue perfectly, but after talking it over with him you have some serious doubts about your own knowledge.

Pro tip: Ask carefully-worded, specific questions.

I'VE CONSTRUCTED A GRAPH TO FURTHER CONFUSE YOU

MANSTRACTION

White noise and detritus that make it virtually impossible to remember why you were in involved with this project in the first place.

MANAGE

To take over a project that someone else was working on without prior explanation or communication.

MANPOSITY

He is frustrated with everyone and somehow still can't figure out that he is the problem.

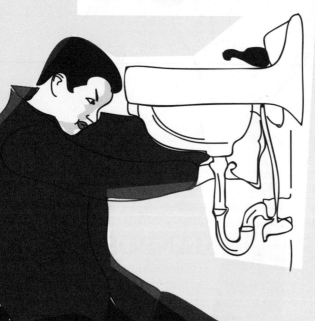

MANGINEERING

It used to work perfectly. Then he tried to fix it and now it doesn't work at all.

Pro tip: Stay out of his way. You can always fix it later.

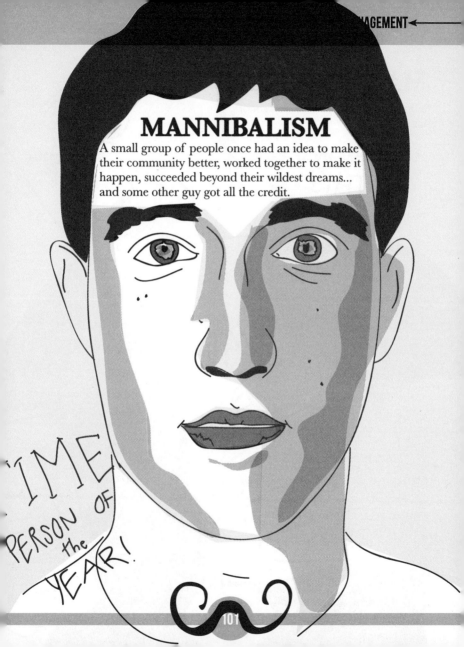

MANNIBALISM

A small group of people once had an idea to make their community better, worked together to make it happen, succeeded beyond their wildest dreams... and some other guy got all the credit.

'IME PERSON OF the YEAR!

MANNOVATION

Seriously, nobody has ever thought of this one before.

MANSISTENCE

He is here to save the day!

MANSTRUCTION

"Here, I'll teach you how to do it....
just move over and let me show you."

Pro tip: This is a strong case for separatism.

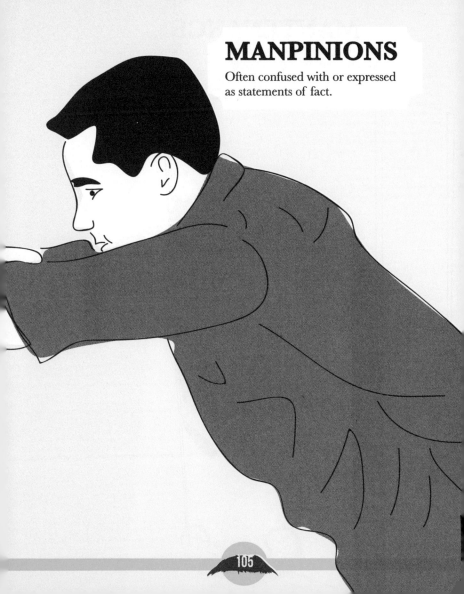

MANPINIONS

Often confused with or expressed as statements of fact.

MANTENANCE

The ability to keep a machine or organization
running perpetually, but badly.

MAGMANIMOUS

The competition is fierce, which is why it's all the more important for him to mantain a generous and forgiving image.

SOCIETAL COLLAPSE
IMMINENT

MANSPLOITATION

The harsh reality that everyone, everywhere is secretly out to get men.

MANTASTIC

1. So far removed from reality that it qualifies as science fiction.
2. Achieving extraordinary results. For men.

MANSPIRACY

Lacking concrete problems, he has ample leisure to imagine complicated scenarios aimed at promoting his suffering.

MANCHURIAN

A conquered man's spirit, dismantled for purposes of control, exploitation, and further study.

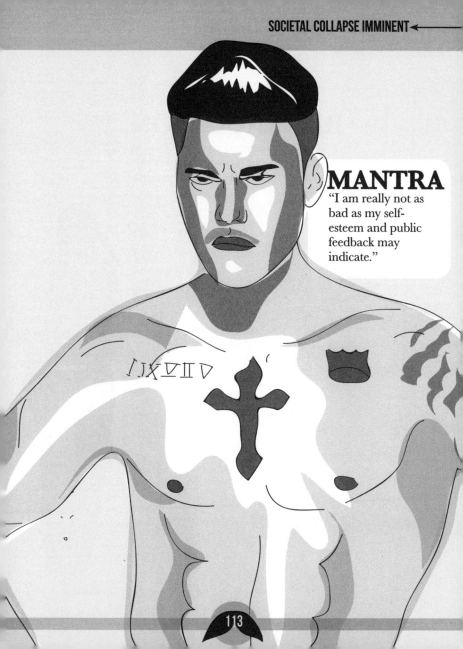

MANTRA

"I am really not as bad as my self-esteem and public feedback may indicate."

REMANCIATION

1. You finally realize that it's easier to reject what you know to be true and right for you.
2. Your white flag response to manspressions.

Pro tip:
It's not you, it's him.

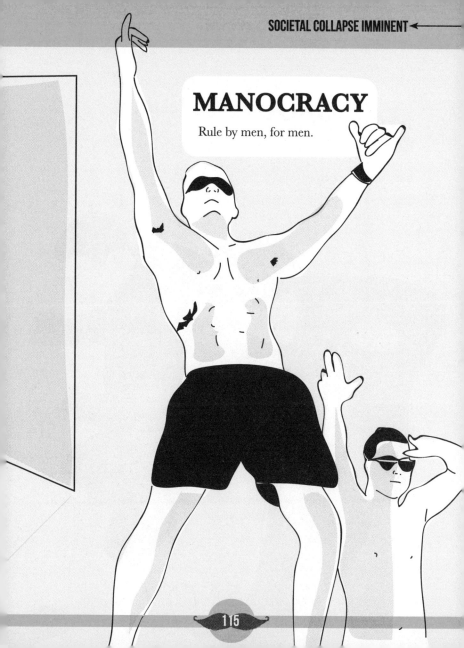

MANOCRACY

Rule by men, for men.

MANARCHY

Rule by the people, for men.
No leaders. No hierarchy. Just
men, acting as perfect equals.

MENINISM

The deep-seated belief that men have the same social, political, and economic rights as other genders.

FUNDAMANTALISM

A form of scripture that upholds strict, inalienable rights of men to mansbehave as they please.

see page 120

MANATICISM

Not even the most oppressive feminism can prevent him from standing up for his rights and those of his fellow men.

MANSBEHAVIOR

Cartoonish overuse of manspression.

MANSGOTIATION

A long negotiation with the end result being his attainment of all of his goals and wishes, and all of your needs being set aside for the time being, of course.

MENDACITY
Untruthfulness

MANDOCTRINATION

Social conditioning leading to the repetition of manspressive forms by those who stand to gain nothing from them.

Pro tip: Be aware, be very aware.

MANCHALANCE

Fear of manspression.

AFTERWORD

(This time we're serious.)

We all do this stuff. Some of us more than others, but really, manspression is the coin of the realm. It's all part of getting by or getting ahead. It's how you express and hold onto power, wealth, and status. Unfortunately, it's also part of what's wrecking our lives.

So what's a person of any gender to do?

We recommend laughter, of course. And when you're done laughing we believe that naming behaviors as you witness them can be helpful and provide better understanding, transparency, and accountability about what goes on around you every day. You'll find yourself in learning and teaching moments but also in difficult thought and conversations about what is driving the subconscious decisions that produce these behaviors.

Please do your best to continue to laugh at the mansbehaviors and manstitutions of the world—but not at the individuals using them. We have not compiled this list in order to taunt, terrorize, or turn the tables, and we urge you not to use either this physical book or the contents within it as a weapon, but rather to be more aware when you encounter these ladder-climbing behaviors.

But knowledge is power. When we can accurately (and catchily) name the stuff that's troubling us, it's much easier to stop it, sidestep it, understand why others might employ it, but also how doing so affects all of us... and most importantly to avoid doing it yourself.

It is the responsibility of each of us to decide how to act, how to treat each other, and how to treat ourselves. But one of the great mandependences of our world is the overreaching of that boundary of *responsibility*. So much burden is placed on individual behavior that if we cannot personally fix all the problems of the world, and control all of the harmful or ill-advised behaviors of others, then it can seem overwhelming and best not to try. So these are ways where you can start small, recognize, and actually begin to change the world around you.

We, of course, urge you to go for it. You can't prevent a person from mansplaining, but you can control your own reaction and influence those around you in how they respond.

And that's priceless.

Elly and Joe

SEND YOUR OWN MAN FAIL TO

PO Box 14332 Portland, OR 97293

(And it may appear in the sequel, *Mansploitation*)

SUBSCRIBE TO EVERYTHING WE PUBLISH!

Do you love what Microcosm publishes?

Do you want us to publish more great stuff?

Would you like to receive each new title as it's published?

Subscribe as a BFF to our new titles and we'll mail them all to you as they are released!

$10-30/mo, pay what you can afford. Include your t-shirt size and month/date of birthday for a possible surprise! Subscription begins the month after it is purchased.

microcosmpublishing.com/bff

...AND HELP US GROW YOUR SMALL WORLD!